USENET: THE ULTIMATE GUIDE

ANONYMITY AND USENET

LANCE HENDERSON

COPYRIGHT

Copyright 2019 Lance Henderson. All Rights Reserved.

CHAPTER 1

Chapter 1: What is Usenet?

You've probably heard the term "Usenet" floating around various tech forums of one flavor or another. Some liken the technology as being similar to P2P, while others state that it is nothing like P2P. In truth, it has a little bit of both systems in that

1.) you can find almost any kind of file therein, such as mp3s, games, movies and the like and

2.) you have the ability to upload and download anything you like

Since its inception in 1979 by two Duke graduate students, Usenet has leapt beyond all expectations in regards to not only data retention, but enhancing freedom of speech. Whereas users were once inundated with extra charges per month for downloading a handful of data, they now have the ability to download terabytes per month, and pay ridiculously small sums to do so. This has all been done with the help of not only thousands of server farms across the world, but also by legions of longtime Usenet users who upload (and leech) every kind of data file in existence. Thus, the true ingredients for the worldwide success of Usenet hasn't been so much because of Usenet providers themselves, but by end-user subscribers who faithfully upload the latest movie, game and music releases every month to the over 100,000 available newsgroups on Usenet.

What typically happens when the average Joe off the street wants to subscribe to Usenet? He usually ends up test driving a free trial by one of the dozens of Usenet providers for a period of two weeks, and then like any P2P user, they are hooked for life. Or at least, the life of the subscription....and that subscription will likely last a long time. Why? The answer lies in the perceived value of the goods he acquires through said Usenet subscription. As mentioned, the worth of the goods acquired far outweighs the monthly fee of the Usenet provider. There are over 100,000 newsgroups, with the large majority of them being TEXT groups rather than BINARY groups (i.e. where the real meat of Usenet is stored). The dirty little secret among long-time Usenet users is this: Usenet would not be one-tenth as popular as it is if it weren't for the bulk of groups like alt.binaries.boneless, alt.binaries.hdtv and alt.binaries.complete_cd. One could make the argument that text discussions certainly have their place that benefits society in some manner, however the bottom line is that file sharing (again, mp3s, movies and games) make up the bulk of not only Usenet, but is the reason Usenet companies have been able to grow their businesses at exponential rates.

<u>Risk vs. Reward? Usenet vs. P2P</u>

If you've paid attention to the news media outlets over the past ten years, you're probably aware of the inherent risks associated with using P2P systems like Emule, Limewire and the like in acquiring copyrighted material. When you fire up a P2P program like Emule, you participate in downloading with your IP address out in the open, from which peers run by law enforcement (i.e. NordicMule) or the Recording Industry can monitor the source and destination with every file you transmit through the network. P2P in effect requires its participants to upload as well as download. It is not so different than downloading torrents in this regard. Usenet on the other hand, encourages leeching without uploading. While you certainly have the freedom to upload, your download speeds are not crippled if you decide only to lurk and leech from the uploads of others. What is more, you do so at your full internet speed, unlike peer-to-peer systems, where you are often at the mercy of others in the swarm.

When someone uploads a copyrighted film (Avengers, for instance) on a p2p or torrent system, it is far easier to track said uploader to an ip address which leads straight to their front door. If however the uploader used a premium Usenet provider to upload the film, the movie industry lawyer must first get his subscriber information from the Usenet company them before any action is taken. If he accessed his Usenet account through a vpn provider, and used anonymous means to pay for his Usenet account, then that adds a further layer of privacy that the entertainment industry lawyers will have to peel back in order to reveal his identity. We'll discuss later on the fruitfulness of signing up anonymously with Usenet and Vpn providers.

To Summarize:
    Pros to Usenet:

- Not dependent on seeders like torrents

- Uses full bandwidth available on your internet connection
- MPAA (Movie Industry), RIAA (Recording Industry) cannot see your downloads as they can with torrents
- Can utilize SSL to encrypt data en route to your pc (unlike torrents)
- In its 30 year history, no one has ever been sued for downloading anything off Usenet (again, unlike with torrents)

Cons to Usenet:

- requires a paid subscription to access older posts
- posting/reading comments require a newsreader/not as easily accessible as torrent sites

Signing up for Usenet

For users who value privacy

For those who are simply not concerned about privacy, you may confidently resist the upselling offers of your Usenet provider's advertisements regarding SSL. At signup for some of the lesser known Usenet providers, the advertising might incline you to believe that you absolutely have to have SSL as an option, otherwise your PC will certainly be hacked by all manner of gremlins, evil gnomes and other bogeymen. Do not believe it. SSL often comes free with a subscription to the major providers, however some providers will still charge extra for it.

For users who value anonymity

Some Usenet providers accept bitcoins as a method of payment. If you are going to be uploading a large amount of legally questionable files and are based in the US, it might be prudent to sign up anonymously for a Usenet account. Do not use any kind of payment that carries personal information about you, such as your name, bank and the like.

Isn't Uploading to Usenet Anonymous with SSL Enabled?

The answer to this question is: sort of. Yes, you can download with impunity. Yes, it encrypted the data in route to your pc, from which point it is decrypted with the decryption key. Most Usenet providers do not keep download logs of what you siphon from the binary Usenet newsgroups. However, the catch is that if you upload, certain information is left as breadcrumbs to your Usenet account. Your messages, in addition to your uploads (all of them) contain unique header identification breadcrumbs, so to speak. If for instance you were part of some conspiracy group of assassins and shouted in some obscure newsgroup that you were going to assassinate the president of the United States, then the Secret Service could look at your headers and find out from the Usenet provider where you lived if you did not sign up anonymously. The nntp posting host & X-Trace lines accomplish this as it often relays the identity of the Usenet server, which in turn leads to your specific account. The Secret Service would have no idea that YOU posted it, but they would know you used Astraweb or Easynews to post it. They in all probability would not even need a subpoena for subscriber information, as most of the big Usenet providers would gladly provide subscriber information that involved terrorist threats, illegal porn or identity fraud (spam is a bit more involved, but then again, the Secret Service doesn't investigate Usenet spam).

There also exists the possibility that the header could be encrypted by the Usenet server themselves, in which case it can only be decrypted by them. The header might have some lengthy mosaic of jumbled letters mixed in with numbers. It might say "sdauhjk7tt324-=asdsad", which of course would be unreadable to anyone except the Usenet provider, as they hold the decryption key and no other Usenet provider does. It is somewhat similar in concept to the headers from a free email service such as Yahoo or Hotmail. This is how the hacker who pried into vice-presidential candidate Sarah Palin's email was arrested: by revealing the headers in the address bar. The FBI took this information from a screenshot the hacker had posted and traced it back to the source. A vpn service would not have helped in such a scenario, since they themselves are bound by the law, and most of them reside in the US anyway. The only way he would have gotten away with it (that is, bragging via a screenshot of her email account with the header exposed) is if he had used Tor to do so from step one. Ironically enough, it seems that a hacker's worst enemy is himself.

Recommended binary newsgroups worth exploring:

Alt.binaries.hdtv: This is perhaps the quintessential newsgroup that carries almost any kind of high definition material you could ever want. Documentaries, mainstream films, tv shows and the like can be found here free for the taking. Be aware that many movies here tend to be passworded. Thus, it is prudent to download the first rar file of the set, extract it, and preview it. Winrar will complain that it is broken, but extract it anyway. You'll get a ten minute preview of the film, or it will complain about the lack of a password entered. Some passwords can only be gained from private forums. If you see a movie you desperately want from the group, but was passworded, ask which forum you can join to extract the file.

Alt.binaries.hdtv.x264: Don't want to have to wait for eons for a 50 gigabyte movie to download from the hdtv group above? Try its sister group, which is a group dedicated to re-encodes of most of the popular movie and tv titles. Re-encoders will take a fifty gigabyte movie and compress it down to an 8-12 gigabyte file, preserving much of the picture quality of the original fifty gigabyte movie. Not recommended if you watch HD on a projector or own a tv that is 42′ inches and above. However for those with a 27′ inch monitor/tv, you will not see much difference as long as the encoder has done a decent job.

Alt.binaries.boneless: This is an all-around depositing group where all manner of files can be uploaded. Anything and everything gets dumped here, and is one of the largest groups on Usenet. Only recommended to those with very fast internet connections, as the header count often takes over an hour on an average connection. Most of the group carries everything you can imagine, which admittedly can be quite jarring for newcomers as there doesn't seem to be any "one" topic for the group.

Alt.binaries.movie.divx: This group is much like the hdtv groups, however few movies are here in HD, saving the downloader hours worth of downloading time. If you're not sure if a film is worth owning, it might prove prudent to test-drive it first with a much smaller size. Most movies here are in the one to two gigabyte size range which is sufficient for a laptop or phone, but you'll notice a substantial difference on a 28 inch monitor as opposed to a dvd with a decent bitrate.

Alt.binaries.sounds.mp3.blues: (substitute your favorite genre instead of blues, such as celtic, jazz, new-age, rock, heavy-metal, classical, christian, etc). Be aware than many of the mp3 groups have strict posting guidelines in their faqs, and will report you to your usenet provider if you spam said groups with off-topic mp3s. However, they offer a very narrowly-defined listening experience depending on your favorite musical tastes

Alt.binaries.games: The main group for posting pc-related games, yet some console game get posted here rather than their specified groups. Be weary of viruses in this group, irregardless of how big the file is. A good anti-virus program is paramount if you are going to be downloading from this group with any regularity. Disable "autoplay" in your operating system, as many a game iso will, when mounted, launch a virus at the first execution of the windows autoplay feature. The iso format itself is not to blame, but rather the file that lie within the folders themselves on the disc image can be virulent.

Alt.binaries.dox: missing an nfo file for a game? This is the place to ask. Game manuals are also uploaded here, along with most every nfo file you can imagine from every "scene" group in existence.

<u>A word of caution concerning binary groups</u>: You will not see much philosophical discussion in these "binaries" groups, aside from bickering about broken rars/not enough pars and endless requests. If you want political or academic debate, subscribe to the lengthy list (there are thousands) of alt groups that do not have "binaries" in the title.

CHAPTER 2

Chapter 2: How to use Usenet

Over the past ten years, Usenet companies have made significant progress in simplifying what was originally a very cumbersome process for Usenet customers. After subscribing to a Usenet provider, it is now ridiculously simple to access the treasures that Usenet holds.

Basics of Using Newsgroups

Downloading: When you sign up for a ten dollar/month plan, your NSP (Newsgroup Service Provider) will email you three things: your username, password, and news address for the server (i.e. news.astraweb.com as an example). There are many different Usenet tools available that are similar in function to how a browser works. You can opt for the simpler method, which requires downloading an .nzb file from free sites like Binsearch, NZBIndex, or Newzbin (paid) and then importing to a newsreader or downloader of your choice. One of the simplest is an app called Nzb-o-Matic

Plus. In the options screen of the application, just insert your user/pass combo and the server address with port 119, then set a destination where your downloads should reside. You can even choose the desktop. It's that simple. There are other free newsgroup tools available as well.

Newshosting Client (requires signup) Free

The Newshosting client self-repairs files for you if you have a subscription to them. However this is a bit redundant since Quickpar and Winrar are free.

Easynews Web Interface (requires signup) Free

The Easynews Interface is similar to the Newshosting client in that you can see thumbnails of the files posted, if they are passworded, and will check for errors automatically.

NewsBin Pro $20

SABnzbd Free

NewsLeecher $20

Binreader Free

GrabIt Free

Unison $29.99

EZ Global Search $2.99

NZB-O-MATIC Plus: Free

Nzb-o-Matic is perhaps the easiest out of all of the above tools to hop aboard Usenet. It is for downloading only however, but once you have the NZB file, you simply import, set your username/pass and download away.

Uploading is a bit trickier, but by no means are you required to upload anything to Usenet. In fact, leeching is encouraged, unlike torrents. If you are new to Usenet, be aware that anything you upload outside of a private proxy or Tor will leave your IP address exposed. Take care if you are unsure if your uploads are copyrighted or not. As they say, luck favors the prepared.

How to Upload to Usenet: (if you have no intention of uploading, skip this)

The process of uploading a small file is not extraordinarily different than uploading a large file. The main difference is that uploading a large file, say gigabytes in size, takes hours on a slow DSL connection. Nevertheless, let's go through some admittedly simplified steps on how to do so. You'll need some free tools to do so, though these are fairly mandatory to the entire process. They are:

Winrar – for archiving the files. You can't upload a single 25 gigabyte Blu-Ray movie to Usenet without risking it failing or timing out. Thus, it is better to use Winrar to break up your movie file in small chunks and upload those. You would be pretty angry if you spent two days downloading a Blu-Ray file only to find out that it "skips" in the middle of the film. Thus, Winrar and Quickpar solve this problem by testing the authenticity for broken parts. Once you have Winrar installed, right click on the file and select "Add to Archive" from the Winrar context menu. Winrar adds this to the windows context menu, thus with a simple right click you can archive any file no matter the size. Just be sure and choose an appropriate size to upload. One hundred megabyte chunks is sufficient for anything over 1 gigabyte in size. Smaller files like mp3s usually are fine with the mp3s non-archived, but will come with par files to repair any redundancies/errors in them. When downloaders finish downloading all the rar pieces, they can right click on any of the posted rars and choose "extract here" to the present directory, or any directory they wish. Before they do this however, they will likely run Quickpar first to check for errors, provided YOU have uploaded pars alongside the rar files of your movie.

Download Winrar at:
   http://www.rarlabs.com/download.htm

Quickpar – for creating par files. This is not mandatory for Usenet uploads (unless the newsgroup specifically asks for it...check their faq), but can be quite a godsend for downloaders as often Usenet servers will "hiccup" during the upload process. Creating parts at 10% redundancy is sufficient for most files.

Download Quickpar at:
   http://www.quickpar.org.uk/Download.htm

Camelsystem Powerpost (Windows only) - A freeware tool used to upload the rar and par files you created. It is delightfully simple to use. You will need your username and password combo from your Usenet provider, along with the port number to insert into the settings menu before your are allowed to upload.

Download Powerpost at http://powerpost.camelsystem.nl/e-index.php

NZB Files – You can think of NZB files as being similar to torrent files that you load into a downloader program. Only instead of using uTorrent, you would import the file into something like Nzb-o-Matic Plus. The NZB file itself is the files you have selected from a site such as Binsearch or NZBindex. It can contain any number of pointers to the files you want, which may be in separate newsgroups. Using an NZB file makes it exponentially easier to manage the files you want, versus those you don't want. In the old days of Usenet, you had to use an archaic program like Agent or Nomad News to manually checkmark each rar or item in separate newsgroups to download what you wanted. This process alone could take an hour or more depending on how many files you wanted. When NZB files came along, they simplified a needlessly cumbersome process of getting what you wanted from your favorite newsgroups.

Incomplete Files – Incomplete Usenet files may look complete in your newsreader, but upon downloading the complete set, you discover that Winrar spits out an error midway through extracting the files. This is usually because the uploader has an unstable connection, or perhaps the power went out upon uploading his files, or a server hiccupped during transmission. Usenet servers transfer files from other Usenet servers, and it differs somewhat than your regular run-of-the-mill internet server. For this reason, you should install the free Quickpar program to alleviate any potential headaches this can cause.

SFV Files – SFV files can be used to verify that your downloaded file is what it is supposed to be, and if any corruption occurred along the way. It doesn't repair the file. That is what Quickpar does. This method of repair is quite different (and yet more stable) than what you might be accustomed to using BitTorrent, where pars are rarely provided with seeded files.

CHAPTER 3

Chapter 3
Usenet Reviews - The Wheat and the Chaff

If you scout around the major search engines and use search terms like "usenet" "best usenet prices" and "usenet reviews", you will literally come across hundreds of websites all clamoring for your referral dollars as they tell you which Usenet provider is best and which ones to avoid. The thing is, most of them offer the exact same services, and by and large are just as competent as the next company. They offer similar services, ease of use, and some like Newshosting even offer their own Usenet browser that will do all of the hard work for you. Almost all of them offer free SSL and unlimited packages as well. Usenet-Server and Astraweb seem to be the cheapest, though Astraweb has had its share of problems regarding incomplete uploads in the past.

For the purposes of anonymity, going with a US based newsgroup provider probably isn't conductive to good anonymity practice. While it certainly isn't foolproof to have an account with a European provider if one is uploading copyrighted material to Usenet (or any other illegal activity), the laws in the US are more litigious and draconian than any other country on Earth that houses the server farms of Usenet companies.

The Big Five

Astraweb: Often the cheapest priced out of all Usenet providers with unlimited specials at $11, their past problems have been server downtime as well as incomplete files (as of 2012). Posted PAR files will certainly make up the difference...most of the time. However on a dual core fitted pc, quickpar can take more than an hour if a sufficiently large amount of rars are broken. In addition, their customer service is not as refined as say, Easynews or Newshosting, but they cannot be beat for the price they offer. If you don't mind a few broken files and using Quickpar on a semi-weekly basis, and price is a concern, Astraweb is the prime choice.

Usenet Server: Similar to Astraweb but more stable infrastructure. They are also a few dollars more in price however for their unlimited plan. Incompletes were not seen in over two years of using them. Thus, you really see where this extra few dollars per month went: system retention and reliability.

Newshosting: Similar to Usenet-Server, however they provide a free newsreader that makes it ridiculously easy to see which files are authentic and which are viruses/spam (hint: look at the file size...if it is a heinously small size, it is probably spam or malware). The thumbnail view is similar to what you would see with Easynews' web interface that scans the thumbs of all the newsgroups you need to view.

Easynews: One of the first companies out of the gate, and one which still does not have the unlimited offerings of the above Usenet providers. However, they are dirt cheap, have a reliable backbone of server farms since they have been in business for eons, and have one of the top forums for troubleshooting and tech issues in the industry. Their customer service is unrivaled as well. The only caveat is that if you are a power user who wants to download over a hundred gigabytes worth of data per month, they probably should not be your first choice. They are, like Giganews, extremely strict with takedown notices from lawyers. If HBO specials and documentaries are your cup of tea, be aware that they have the ability to "nuke" uploads should they deem it too "hot" to reside on their servers (i.e. Game of Thrones, The Sopranos, etc)

Giganews: Undoubtedly the most expensive of all the Usenet premium providers. They provide one of the largest server backbones, and provide similar services as the above mentioned providers. They are considered the "Harvard" of Usenet companies, however it seems rather needless to pay for the name since you get most of the benefits from the other big four Usenet companies. Giganews is also known for giving in to "take down" requests for uploaders of copyrighted content, such as HBO series like Game of Thrones, in which files were purged from the servers in such a large quantity as to make pars useless to recover them. The problem therein, is that many smaller Usenet companies use Giganews backend servers for access to Usenet. Thus, when they do comply with a take down order or request from some Hollywood law firm, other Usenet providers are affected. If money is not an issue, Giganews is a great choice for their consistently good customer service.

Others: Thundernews, Newsdemon, Ngroups, etc.

You're taking a spin on the roulette wheel with anyone not in the top five. That is not to say they all provide bad service, but it is important to note that a rock-solid business like those in the top five take years and years of backbreaking work and perseverance. The lesser known Usenet providers usually are lacking one of three key areas: customer service (usually emails from tech support), reliability/completion of files, or retention (age of files). Some of them are so newly minted that they have no choice but to rent part of their infrastructure from the likes of Giganews or Highwinds, which have many, many server farms.

In the end you might ask, what is the number one thing that customers want from a Usenet provider? It is not retention. Most Usenet companies have similar retention rates that span many years. It is not even completion of files. Most large uploads from users around the world upload a sufficient number of pars to repair any large group of posted files such as Blu-Ray movies or the like. No, what Usenet customers most want is GOOD CUSTOMER SERVICE. Customers don't want to sit waiting on the phone up to an hour for tech support to answer. To wit, they want someone who speaks the same language and in the same dialect. They also don't want to be spammed with upselling offers by the Usenet company in question (web hosting companies like Godaddy are notorious for this), nor do they like to be called on the phone with such offers.

The First Rule of Usenet (don't talk about Usenet!)

On many social media sites and forums such as Facebook, Twitter and Reddit, some users will post advertisements from the late nineties from such big box stores as BestBuy, Wal-Mart, Sears and the like that show a dramatic difference in regards to hardware costs. For example, a 1.5

gigabyte hard drive from BestBuy in 2000 cost over $200 dollars. Now however, for the same amount of dollars you can buy a 3 terabyte drive. It is not that different for Usenet server farms. As time goes by and more customers sign on for premium Usenet accounts, the business costs incurred for Usenet companies goes down. That is why you can have an unlimited data account for less than ten dollars a month. So then, why is traditional file-sharing such as torrenting more popular?

The reason is because it is eminently easier to download a torrent for free than it is to fish out your credit card and set up a Usenet account. Ridiculous, is it not? It is also easier to see comments on a torrent site than read and filter through all the spam in a Usenet newsgroup such as alt.binaries.boneless. Some interfaces, such as Newshosting's newsgroup browser will filter out most of the spam and passworded files and make it easier to use.

It is a well-known fact by most BitTorrent users that the Record and Movie industries like to unleash their armies of lawyers upon copyright works that have seeds numbered in the millions. This makes it very convincing in a lawsuit as far as who you uploaded files with and to whom you didn't. Often, a movie release for September might be leaked in August, and the swarm of users will catch the attention of the copyright holders and sue the downloaders as well as uploaders provided their true ip address is showing. This is less the case with Usenet, where it is not possible to see who downloaded which file, even in casting a wide net. Thus, if you live in a litigious society like that in the United States, it is to your benefit to learn to utilize Usenet's strengths in this regard.

On many forums you will hear users say "Usenet is dead" or "Usenet doesn't have what torrents have". Take confidence in the fact that people who espouse such nonsense don't in fact use Usenet themselves. It is not beyond the realm of impossibility that such naysayers are actually attorneys, or employee shills for the record industry who don't want legions of potential Usenet experts asking too many questions concerning what it has to offer.

CHAPTER 4

Chapter 4: Usenet Anonymity

In this chapter, we'll discuss ways you can add anonymity to your Usenet connection, so that you can participate in discussion groups without fear of persecution. These methods often are most useful in situations where you may lose your Usenet account if you say the wrong things to the wrong people. Usenet companies are big business now, and unlike twelve years ago, will now think nothing of terminating your account of they get enough complaints. Simply being unpopular and taking a stand against the status quo in certain newsgroups can get your Usenet account banned (i.e. alt.privacy). However, with true anonymity, they may ban your account, but rest assured that not only will your words remain forever on Usenet, but you will not be persecuted for speaking out against a tyrannical government, or a company that you work for (which has happened many times by disgruntled employees on Facebook).

It should be stated at the outset that using Tor for Usenet binary downloads will actually strain the Tor network, just as it does with torrents. And to boot, whenever you use torrents via Tor, the torrent software actually sends your IP address to the recipient. It does so anonymously, in the same way a post office worker will deliver you your mail. Needless to say this defeats the purpose of using torrents. This problem is not with the Tor code, but rather the way that applications like BitLord and BitTorrent are designed. The torrent applications themselves need to be coded to allow anonymity. It is better to use Freenet with the Frost addon for p2p-like trading if you wish to remain anonymous. Tor is much more efficient at textual discussions and binary downloaders using your native connection, but the easiest method to do this anonymously is by use of the remailer network. By using such a method, the identifying Usenet posts are stripped away from your messages, essentially erasing the digital trail that leads back to your IP address.

As we have seen from past media reports around the world over the last several years, there could be any number of valid reasons you want to hide your identity.

- Maybe you work for a computer manufacturer, or perhaps a robotics company and are concerned about the lack of safety measures being enforced by your superiors, but fear some kind of retaliation by them should you go public, like the loss of your job. Usenet is a great place to ask advice and not worry about the consequences. Places like Facebook and Twitter on the other hand might invite retribution by the executives or CEO of your company.

- It could be that you want to vocally protest your discontent with the direction of the prevailing winds of government. Doing so in countries like the US, Iran, China, and the like could put you on a "watch" list of sorts, and before you know it, you have problems relating to "no fly" lists at airports and border stations.

- Perhaps you want to establish a free email address that has never had any contact whatsoever with your real IP address. Services like Yahoo Mail, Gmail, and Hotmail repeatedly scan emails looking for keywords or files in which to flag. Shutting down your email is one thing. Having your IP address along with the email forwarded to government entities for prosecution is quite another. Anonymity prevents this from happening.

Remailers

As a crude example, let's say you own a reporting agency that is active in most of the less-than-savory newsgroups, and you use your email from your office quite regularly. Then you see a rape victim who needs your assistance. You might not want to divulge your email address to everyone. Using a remailer will ensure that any identifying information of you will be erased from the headers of any messages you upload to newsgroups. Your message will be forwarded to the recipient without any risks of public disclosure.

Traceable vs. Untraceable Remailers

Traceable: there are some types of remailers that keep active lists of senders/pseudonyms whereby receivers can reply to mail by fictitious names. When the remailer gets a message, it consults a list and forwards mail to the sender. Thus, there is an element of privacy to this method of communication; however as was proved in previous years by the penet.fi (Finland) incident, this does not provide anonymity. Any hacker, government agency, judge, or the like can gain access to said list and discover who the sender is. In the case of penet.fi, Scientology launched a lawsuit of copyright infringement against them, in which a lower court demanded they turn over the identity of its users.

Untraceable: If no list is maintained on the pseudonyms of users, then security is increased exponentially...provided you are willing to give up two way communications with your party. Needless to say, this has some drawbacks, and is in some ways inferior to using Tor and/or PGP to communicate. In addition, there is always the possibility of hacker attacks whereby once entry is gained upon the server, anonymity is compromised. Traffic-sniffers along with a host of other tools can also be used as a method of attack, as they compare and contrast the traffic emanating from the server. Such attacks are very difficult to coordinate, but are somewhat analogous to attacks within Tor and also Freenet, whereby if a sufficiently high number of hostile nodes are controlled within the network, then probability of stripping away layers of anonymity becomes more likely. In other words, if Law Enforcement for instance, controls all Tor relays, the long-term effect would be similar if they had control of most nodes on Freenet. Though they are admittedly vastly different technologies, they do share one common goal: hiding the true IP address of senders and recipients.

Mixmaster techniques however attempt to thwart such subversive attempts by sending messages through several servers across the globe, in various countries of legality and law enforcement jurisdictions. It becomes exponentially difficult for hackers and/or government entities to bunny hop from server-to-server across the globe in order to track down where the original sender resided. Thus, it goes well above and beyond the phrase "don't put all your eggs in one basket" and is more akin to "many eggs, many baskets". Such is the skeletal framework of the onion-routing network Tor.

You may download Mixmaster here.

Things That Break Anonymity on Usenet

1.) <u>Giving out your real email address</u>, even one from one of the "free" services such as Yahoo, Hotmail and the like, not only can, but *will* open you up to armies of spambots, guaranteed. You would be surprised at how many new to Usenet are under the impression that these free email services are somehow foolproof to the legions of bots that trawl Usenet. A better alternative: use a fictional name and temporary "Usenet-Only" email. If you have a website, your host probably offers you the ability to create throwaway accounts. Or, go with Anonymizer Nyms at https://www.nyms.net for twenty bucks per year. SharpMail, Mailinator & Hushmail are also excellent options, however if you want anonymity as well as privacy, remember to sign up while on the Tor network, not the open web. Also remember not to use credit cards or paypal, as it leaves a money trail. Better to use Bitcoins or a money order with no link back to you.

2.) <u>Dropping Personal Info</u>. This is a big one, and one that is seen quite frequently on various groups where flame wars erupt over issues like political campaigns, privacy and even some mp3 groups (i.e. alt.binaries.sounds. mp3.electronic). Political affiliations/liaisons, favorite restaurants, bars, musical groups and the like can lead to some stalker building a profile on you, then hopping on Facebook, Twitter or LinkedIn and keying in all the personal data you have given over the past six months. Remember that whatever is typed in *any* newsgroup will be there for years and years. Type in "labor" as "labour" or "color" as "colour", and it is not difficult to discern your country of origin.

3.) <u>Leaving messages with your headers clearly visible</u> to the reading public. By using various search tools, they can see every message you posted to Usenet, even if you used different nyms. This of course doesn't occur if you use a service that strips away this information.

4.) <u>Signing up for a Usenet or VPN service using credit cards</u>

Realize that when you use your credit card to purchase anything like a vpn (virtual private network) or Usenet account, you are in fact leaving a money trail straight to your identity. If you are only after a small measure of privacy, such as wanting a Usenet account that doesn't monitor/log your downloads, then a vpn is fine. However if it is anonymity you want, you will have to sign up for *both* Usenet as well as the vpn service using anonymous means, either by bitcoins, money order, or a prepaid debit card with no identifying information leading back to you.

Truecrypt, Usenet and Passwords

In all of this talk of posting rars, pars and messages out in the open newsgroups, it would be a shame not to mention that you can also upload locked containers and encrypted volumes to Usenet as well. The main difference is that you have to have the Truecrypt (free) application installed, and create an encrypted container with messages or data therein before uploading it to a Usenet newsgroup. There are lots of different newsgroups that allow this and many that don't. However you can use alt.binaries.test as a means to communicate covertly with another, or share files privately with another person. The encryption is actually fairly straightforward. When you create the Truecrypt container with the data you want to send to someone else, you could then rar that one file (or files) and upload that. Then the only ones who would be privy to its contents are those with the keyfile, which you could email to them, and/or the password to the container.

The benefit of implementing Tor (for text groups, not

binaries), Usenet and Truecrypt simultaneously is that you get the best of both worlds. You get the privacy that a vpn will allow, in addition to having the anonymity (different than privacy) of Truecrypt.

Always check the newsgroup's FAQ first before passwording files as many groups do not allow it. What is the worse that can happen? Your Usenet provider will be inundated with complaints and they will revoke your posting privileges, which can be quite a cumbersome ordeal regardless of whether you have signed up anonymously or not. If in doubt, ask the group, or post the word "passworded" or "pw" in the subject line. Groups like alt.binaries.hdtv, which are flooded with passworded blu-ray files, will thank you for it. There is nothing quite infuriating as downloading a 50 gigabyte Blu-Ray disc and finding out that it won't extract the files because of a password requirement. This is in addition to not having a membership to the forum where such a password was revealed in the first place.

Running Usenet from a mounted Truecrypt image

Optionally, you could create an encrypted volume, install your Usenet newsreader into that container, and only run your newsreader upon the mounting of said container. Just be aware that some applications like to leave temp files in the system drive (C:), but most should have an option to set such a directory (i.e. set it within the encrypted container itself). You will have to mount it to the same letter directory each time if you don't want to change it every session, however it makes it very handy to secure communications privately between you and someone else without the entire newsgroup seeing what you are saying or trading. There may be an instance where you spent a lot of money on a rare, vintage recording of an obscure album, and you don't want anyone else in the mp3 group trying to make money off it on eBay. Solution? Use Truecrypt to encrypt the mp3s. Rar them up with a password and upload to a newsgroup on Usenet.

If you are in a country that makes it difficult to engage in free discussion online, such as Iran, China and the like, make sure that you do not leave your encrypted images running with your Usenet newsreader/browser. Doing so leaves all the data open to any kind of government entity that decides to raid your place of residence. Thus, if you are a regular poster in the group "alt.discussion.tibetan-freedom" it would be wise to not leave your PC running unattended at all, especially with a Truecrypt image mounted and in operation.

PGP and Usenet

You can also use PGP to encrypt messages to newsgroup as well. PGP is a free encryption application similar (however more complex) to Truecrypt. You can encrypt messages from one newsgroup to another, to any recipient you like, and they can in turn decrypt your message. It is more efficient to use PGP for the purposes of covert Usenet communication than it is to use Truecrypt, as the applications are meant for different security scenarios. It should be said that the pgp manual is not an easy read. It will take you some measure of effort to get your head around encrypting/decrypting messages from Usenet, as it is not as straightforward and newbie-friendly as say, Truecrypt. It is worth your time in learning however if you want to exchange encrypted messages with other PGP members on Usenet.

PGP-related newsgroups:
alt.security.pgp
comp.security.pgp.announce
comp.security.pgp.discuss
comp.security.pgp.resources

comp.security.pgp.tech

Technical Sources on Cryptography, Security & Encryption

www.iacr.org – Intern. Association of Cryptologic Research – contains a wealth of data on crypto as well as miscellaneous related security programs

www.pgpi.org – Homepage and Resource for PGP and its applications

www.nist.gov/aes – AES, or Advanced Encryption Standard used by Truecrypt, Drivecrypt, PGP

To moderate or not to moderate Usenet

It would be certainly short-sighted to suggest that Usenet should have total anarchy and no moderation at all. Newsgroups that employ the use of a moderator can have stark advantages over unmoderated groups, so much so that the group attracts far more attention from new users than it would without such moderation. The most glaring problems with a totally unmoderated setting can be seen quite clearly within discussion groups on Freenet, where moderation is not possible. Individual users can opt to "ignore" all posts from certain users on their own, or create their own Frost discussion group with a private encryption key (that is, unless said key is leaked, in which the spammers engage in a full frontal assault on the group). On Freenet, spam, personal attacks, racism and hatred abound, however the responsibility is placed upon the individual to self-censor/delete posts within the group. On Usenet, even moderators have been unsuccessful at completely eradicating spam and personal flame wars between members.

That is not to suggest that a moderator is the equivalent of a Big Brother-like censor, however it makes discussion in the newsgroup more honest and less prone to those who like to derail threads into off-topic discussions. An inherent downside to being a regular on a heavily moderated Usenet newsgroup is that tolerance becomes difficult to maintain.

After years and years of engaging in civil discourse in various groups, a user might find it a bit of a challenge to participate in a group that offers a more relaxed discussion topic structure. In one of the mp3 newsgroups (electronic), untold numbers of flame wars have erupted over the years concerning new users (as well as old) who would post collections of ambient/new-age artists. Now, there are other mp3 groups better suited for collections by, for instance, Michael Stearns. Few electronic music fans would find him suited for the electronic mp3 newsgroup, however every now and then a new Usenet user would show up and mistakenly post to the group his latest offering. He would be summarily crucified with curses, flames and threats to inform his Usenet provider that he was spamming the group. This type of intolerable attitude does more harm than good. There was also many uploads done of artist Steve Roach, whose music transcends several different genres: new-age, ambient, trance and electronic, yet the uploader of said music was similarly cursed and vehemently badgered by long-term users.

CHAPTER 5

Chapter 5: Which VPN companies respect anonymity?

If you are a bit squeamish about accessing Usenet via your local ISP, you can always add an extra layer of privacy by subscribing to a vpn (virtual private network) service close to you. There are a plethora of good vpn providers that will route your internet connection through them and provide ssl (secure socket layer) encryption so that your isp cannot see what you do online. Most all of them use similar technology to achieve this, and have comparable speeds. A vpn service is much, much faster than using an onion-routing network like Tor, but not all of them will tolerate p2p usage. However, they will tolerate a Usenet account.

Unlike Tor, the vpn provider, which usually charges somewhere in the range of ten dollars per month for unlimited service (over and above what you pay your Usenet provider), WILL be able to see everything that you do through their connection, unless you route that connection through the Tor network. They are more tolerable to Usenet than they are P2P systems, as Usenet is less likely to incur a swarm of copyright lawyers sending them angry cease-and-desist letters. Bottom line: some vpns will log your IP, and some won't. If they know your real name and address, you can be sure that law enforcement will (and any other type of law agency) with a subpoena. It's a hit and miss game, and one which seems entirely dependent on whether the provider keeps online logs of the traffic that goes through their portal. One popular vpn provider, BlackVPN, said this in their FAQ:

"Although we do not monitor the traffic, incoming or outgoing connections of our users we may assign users to a unique IP address and log which user was assigned which IP address at a given time. If we receive a copyright violation notice from the appropriate copyright holder then we will forward the violation to the offending user and may terminate their account. We therefore ask our users not to distribute or transmit material which violates the copyright laws in either your country or the country in which our Service is hosted."

The above defeats the entire purpose of anonymity on the internet. A novice who didn't know the difference between privacy and anonymity might conclude from their website that they offered complete anonymity similar to what Tor offers, but that is clearly not the case at all. One has to be quite attentive to the fine details of the advertising on sites such as theirs to see if any logs are kept, and in many cases they will not reveal such information unless you explicitly email them and ask. Interestingly, in 2011 the website TorrentFreak initiated a rather close examination of all of the vpn provider's response to the question "Under what jurisdictions does your company operate and under what exact circumstances will you share the information you hold with a 3rd party?"

Some of the answers were expectantly evasive, and others were quite illuminating. One provider, CryptCloud, said

"We don't log anything on the customer usage side so there are no dots to connect period, we completely separate the payment information. Realistically, unless you operate out of one of the 'Axis of Evil Countries" Law Enforcement will find a way to put the screws to you. I have read the nonsense that being in Europe will protect you from US Law Enforcement, worked well for HMA didn't it? Furthermore I am pretty sure the Swiss Banking veil was penetrated and historically that is more defend-able than individual privacy. The way to solve this is just not to log, period."

Two points to make. One, the HMA (Hide My Ass vpn) incident he refers to involved a member of the hacker group Lulzsec, in which one of their core members was arrested. Two, he cites the "Axis of Evil", but clearly they are not in one of those countries.

The above is not to suggest that their actual service is less than that which they advertise, but the distinction between privacy and anonymity often falls victim to the gnomes who work in the marketing department of said companies. CryptoCloud is located in...San Antonio, Texas, which has one of the most brutally unmerciful judiciary systems in the United States. If a federal judge (or Congress) wanted the identity of one of their customers, you can be sure that such information would be handed over in a heartbeat in order to avoid heavy day-to-day fines. If they are based in the US, they would *have* to have your personal identity information available in order to avoid bankruptcy by the federal government. To wit, this doesn't necessarily have to have anything to do with terrorism, cp, spam or counterfeiting. It could be as simple as running a file sharing server. The case involving Megaupload proves that true anonymity, at least that which is beyond the long arm of the law, is difficult to obtain, even if you reside in another country. Still, it is worth having a vpn account simply because it adds an extra layer of privacy to your sessions. If you are a habitual uploader, you could do a lot worse than to pay ten dollars a month for an extra peace of mind.

The solution? Sign up to a vpn provider anonymously. There are several providers who accept Bitcoins as payment.

http://www.thebitcoinlist.com/dp_internet/vps-vpn/

CHAPTER 6

Chapter 6: The Cloud (the Enemy of Usenet and Anonymity)

It goes without saying that men are voracious collectors of many things obtained online: mp3 collections, digital wallpaper, pdf files and the like. The term "cloud" has been given flighty and unwieldy definitions from one blogger to the next, as if the "cloud" is actually some impenetrable fortress in the digital sky where no moth or thief can break in and corrupt or steal. However secure you feel that your files are "in the cloud", it is perhaps worth remembering that whoever owns the "cloud", owns your stuff. Thus, the cloud is nothing more than a server farm with hundreds of other people's hard drives & servers, all digitally categorizing... your stuff. No longer are your things flying under the banner of privacy in your own home, but rather you are subject to whatever litigious lawyer's terms and conditions contract he has drummed up for the cloud provider. Be wary of a future promised where your data is at the whims of some far away server operator who gets to dictate which of your purchased music, movies and games gets "streamed" to your pc.

The Windows 8 operating system has a feature called "SmartScreen" that is used for checking the validity and safety of files before they are executed. This type of feature was first implemented in Internet Explorer and Windows Live Messenger to thwart malicious sites from being able to exploit people's browsers. Thus, verification and authentication were at the forefront of the feature, as it sought to prevent spam, malware and adware from infecting people's computers. A good thing? Not for the majority of users, who found it rather annoying. It was a one-step-forward, two-steps-backward approach that actually hindered the internet experience for millions of users of Internet Explorer as they attempted to go to links that were not dangerous in the least. Enter Windows 8, in which the SmartScreen feature tries to verify whether applications are "safe" to download or run on the operating system. It checks a dynamic, ever-changing laundry list of exploitable URLs that Microsoft has identified as harmful for end-users on pc systems. An additional problem with this is that it is cumbersome to turn off, and once done, results in consistent nagging from the operating system to re-enable it. Where it will be three to five years down the road? Will you have to have every app or file on your pc "authorized" by Microsoft's servers before you can execute them? What about cloud content and streaming legally purchased items to your own pc?

For the uninitiated, Microsoft likes to assign "download reputation" points to digitally signed websites as well as programs. The problem with this is the same problem that manifests itself in anti-virus programs, namely that a lot of false-positives get thrown in the user's face, leading to frustration and annoyance. At times, downloads will get frozen in Internet Explorer 9 as the downloaded files get scanned. There is no option in Internet Explorer 9 to switch it off and let end-users decide what security setting to implement. Rare files constantly get falsely flagged as being somehow malicious for the pc. There is a further element of privacy intrusion for the SmartScreen feature. It collects data on every program you install on your operating system, and checks to see if a valid certificate exists on Microsoft's "cloud" (i.e. their server) that verifies its "safety" for your operating system. It checks the hash of the program installer itself, and compares it to a list at Microsoft. Think about how many programs you have installed on your pc that are related to privacy: PGP, Truecrypt, BitLocker, the installer your vpn provider emailed you, and perhaps even encrypted keyfiles to your hard drive. It would be a gold mine of epic proportions for any hacker to get at such data.

Enter Usenet. As of 2012, it is relatively easy to hop on Usenet without having to jump through hoops to do so. When you download data from Usenet, it is typically decoded by your newsreader or NZB application and then saved to your hard drive. If you have an anti-virus installed, it most likely will have some element of checking each executable or installer that is downloaded to your pc, either by Usenet or some other variant of internet app. With the rush to maximize the use of cloud computing, however, the responsibility of initializing these types of security settings is slowly being taken away from the end-user. What does this mean for Usenet? One of two things could happen.

1.) Eventually, users stream data off of usenet, which is

then checked and "verified" through an intermediary cloud server, before being delivered to your hard drive (assuming you have one).

2.) Usenet SSL will be prohibitively expensive and/or reserved only for certain groups in society (think Government, Intelligence, etc). Secure, anonymous programs like PGP, Freenet, Truecrypt and the like will be stigmatized and shunned by cloud servers for their inability to unmask and decrypt their true contents.

In 2010, an article titled "The Death of the Hard Drive" explored Google's persistent momentum towards a hard-drive-less selection of flagship products, all citing the benefits of "cloud storage". In 2012, Microsoft is gearing Windows 8 towards such a platter-less scenario.

"Stop worrying about when the hard drive in your computer will die. Google wants to kill it permanently anyway.

The new Google Chrome operating system, which was unveiled Tuesday, as well as hints and suggestions from Apple and Microsoft, offers us a preview of the PC of the future. And it will come without that familiar whirring disk that has been the data heart of the PC for the past 25 years.

The Chrome OS will at first be available on all-black laptops from Samsung and Acer. And because the new platform stores everything — files, applications, data bits and bytes, literally everything — on online servers rather than on your home or office PC, those new PCs running it won't require gobs of storage. In fact, they won't require any storage at all."

Further reasons why you should never rely on the Cloud for your personal data backups.

1.) You are completely at the mercy of your ISP's bandwidth cap. They stand to make a fortune as you stream your own personal mp3s, games, video (which competes with their own brand) and the like to your personal devices. No hard drive means you'll be streaming quite regularly. Bandwidth caps will necessarily cause you to pay more for products that you have paid in full. Thus, true ownership becomes a misnomer. Instead, you will "rent" the products you buy from online digital sources. Usenet prices will go up, as customers will not be able to afford the massive price spikes in bandwidth costs. One of the hallmarks of Usenet premium providers is the "unlimited" package. However what good is "unlimited" when your ISP caps your connection? Many ISPs (especially those in Canada, such as Bell Sympatico) falsely advertise such unlimited options and speeds.

2.) <u>US jurisdiction</u>. Most of the server backbones related to cloud computing reside in the heart of the USA. That means your private data, while in the "cloud", is subject to laws dictated by the US Congress and US Legislature. What is quasi-legal in your own country in the Ukraine, or Timbuktu, might be dastardly illegal in the United States. Some government entities might insist that sites like Amazon not only cancel your account and delete your purchased files on their servers, but relay all personal subscriber information to them for proceedings in an American court. It has happened before. There is also the opportunity for said government agencies (or hackers) to intercept your data streaming down to you to verify its authenticity. For your own good, naturally. Google and Microsoft know what is best for you, right?

3.) <u>Encryption is allergic to Cloud Computing</u>. You can bet the ranch that almost every Cloud Computing server operator will demand to see what is inside encrypted files in order to minimize the risk of being fined by the FCC or investigated by other alphabet agencies like the IRS (taxes), and FBI (fraud/copyright). This is not necessarily the case today, in 2012, but you can be sure that if everyone has absolutely no choice but to upload their digital purchases to their servers, they will want to see the contents of everything since it resides on "their" server cloud. Google, Microsoft and Yahoo repeatedly scan personal emails in an attempt to better target their user's browsing habits with targeted ads. It would be no different for mp3s, videos or love letters contained in encrypted Truecrypt volumes.

4.) It cheapens individuality. The collective group-think that is inherent in the pursuit to herd all the digital sheep into one pen is the anti-thesis of not only privacy and human rights on an individual level, it makes everyone dependent on a single system. In August 2012, Steve Wozniak, co-founder of Apple said at a Washington expose said:

"I really worry about everything going to the cloud. I think it's going to be horrendous. I think there are going to be a lot of horrible problems in the next five years. With the cloud, you don't own anything. You already signed it away. I want to feel that I own things. A lot of people feel, 'Oh, everything is really on my computer,' but I say: the more we transfer everything onto the web, onto the cloud, the less we're going to have control over it."

And Steve would be correct. If Cloud computing takes off the way Google and Microsoft wants, you will find someone else in some other state, province, or country setting the times when you are allowed to access your own data, encrypted or not.

5.) George Orwell's 1984. Maybe it will never quite happen as it is alluded to in the book. Then again, no one could fathom that a Category 5 hurricane would wipe out New Orleans, or that 3000 people would die at the hands of

19 mangy terrorists on Sept. 11th, 2001. For several years now, the US has expressed the desire for an internet "kill switch" to deal with the less than desirable in our society. Today, it is terrorists, spammers and identity thieves. Tomorrow, it is people who obviously have something to hide if they implement SSL in their Usenet setups and upload Truecrypt volumes "to the cloud". It is this kind of slow erosion of private property that forced the hand of Revolution in the 17th and 18th centuries.

The above reasons are sufficient to put a shred of doubt insofar as Usenet usage is concerned. Usenet users rely on their physical hard drives for storage of their data acquired from Usenet, and regardless of what that data is, it would slowly kill the Usenet industry if users had to "stream" their files from their Usenet accounts with no place to securely store them. They also enjoy the privilege of not having their download logs kept by anyone. Such is certainly not true of most torrent trackers, where every seed participating in the swarm reveals their ip address to anyone connected, day or night, for days and weeks on end.

Disregard Authoritarians, Acquire Privacy

To reverse the heavy tide against groupthink and giving up private ownership of your own files (on Usenet, or elsewhere), a stand needs to be taken now, and with more than simply our wallets. There was once a time back in the 1990s where the purveyors of Usenet did not have to worry about their posts being chiseled in stone among the newsgroups which would last for generations. Even one year retention for textual newsgroups was not that common, and five year retention for binaries was but a dream. Many Usenet users weren't afraid to use their real names and real emails in messages. At the time, there was little reason to be. Now however, in addition to the ever-ominous threat of being stalked (and kidnapped/killed)

Every message posted to Usenet is archived by Google (DejaNews/Google Groups) in the same way that they are taking high resolution photos of every nook and cranny upon the earth via Google Earth. The aim of this digital push towards "the Cloud" seems to be to minimize individuality as well as putting an end to privacy. The technology is here that every move you make on the street will be recorded not by security cameras sitting atop state buildings and banks, but by each other. Google has not only recorded every single message posted to Usenet within the last five years, it wants to do something eerily similar with their Project Glass product, in which users will be sold a pair of glasses with a built-in webcam that monitors everything around it, giving immediate data about their surroundings: buildings, restaurants, museums and the like. Only it won't stop there. Eventually it will focus on people, as that is where the ad revenue streams lie. According to Google:

"We think Glass helps you share your life as you're living it; from life's big moments to everyday experiences. Today we're kicking off what we're calling Glass Sessions, where you can experience what it's like to use Glass while we build it, through the eyes of a real person, in real life. The first Glass Session follows Laetitia Gayno, the wife of a Googler, as she shares her story of welcoming a new baby, capturing every smile, and showing her entire family back in France every "first" through Hangouts."

True Security lies with the Individual, not the State

We may come to a point where it may be impossible to truly harbor any anonymity at all on Usenet or anywhere else. Users who don't have the latest "reality enhancer" (which just so conveniently carries every data imaginable about your birth, health, academic & employment history) would suffer severe ostracization from peers (i.e. Facebook defriending, etc)

As anyone with a RAID hard drive setup can attest, technology gets smaller with each generation, and holds infinitely more data the further into the future you progress. There will come a point where you will not need to wear glasses to record and upload your immediate surroundings to the internet. All of the surveillance will inevitably shrink in size to a state where your naked eye will not notice their presence at all. This is what happened with Usenet. No one knew back in the 1990s that everything we said or did online was going to be archived (archive.org) for anyone to peruse decades later.

Thus, we now censor ourselves on Usenet for fear of being reported to whatever authorities can punish us accordingly. Excessive data therefore, is actually the anti-thesis of freedom. Usenet SSL, VPNs, & Tor all provide a power to the end user that is slowly being shunned and minimized by those with the power to do so (i.e. Google, Facebook,). It is certainly not 100% integrated into society yet, but it is coming. To foster more privacy on Usenet, we need more anonymity. People need to be free to speak their minds and engage civil discussion without worrying about the powers that be (Google) pulling the strings of censorship. We will get to the point where we will be accused of "being up to no good" by refusing to play along. Have an encrypted volume and plan to cross the border? The border guard might ask you to decrypt. Refuse and they can confiscate your laptop for five days, making the trip fairly aggravating. Will it one day be considered a capital crime to erase some negative thing about your past history on the internet without some government entity's stamp of approval?

LASTLY...

A small favor...

Thank you friend for buying my book. I'm just a simple church mouse writing these books and as an indie I'd forever appreciate it if you (if you enjoyed it) wrote a nice review so others might learn about anonymity, opsec, usenet, or whatever floats their boat.

Thank you again and May God Bless You on your journey!

Burners & Black Markets

Tor and the Dark Art of Anonymity

Invisibility Toolkit

Darknet: A Beginner's Guide To Staying Anonymous

5 in 1 Darknet Pack (5 books in 1)

Coming Soon:

Burners & Black Markets 2: Good Guys Wear Black

Dark Linux